CORE LIBRARY OF US STATES

California

BY RICHARD SEBRA

CONTENT CONSULTANT
Camille Suarez, PhD
Assistant Professor
Nineteenth Century US History, California History
California State University, Los Angeles

Core Library
An Imprint of Abdo Publishing
abdobooks.com

abdobooks.com

Published by Abdo Publishing, a division of ABDO, PO Box 398166, Minneapolis, Minnesota 55439.

Printed in the United States of America, North Mankato, Minnesota
052022
092022

THIS BOOK CONTAINS RECYCLED MATERIALS

Cover Photo: Shutterstock Images
Interior Photos: Shutterstock Images, 4–5, 17 (flag), 28–29, 31, 33, 34–35, 37, 38, 43; Red Line Editorial, 9 (California), 9 (USA); Eric Paul Zamora/The Fresno Bee/AP Images, 10–11; Robert Fried/Alamy, 13; Martin Mecnarowski/Shutterstock Images, 17 (bear); Thomas Morris/Shutterstock Images, 17 (bird); Joshua Rainey Photography/Shutterstock Images, 17 (tree); Tony Baggett/Shutterstock Images, 17 (flower); Sergey Novikov/Shutterstock Images, 20–21, 45; Allard One/Shutterstock Images, 24; David A. Litman/Shutterstock Images, 26; Javier Garcia/Shutterstock Images, 40

Editor: Marie Pearson
Series Designer: Joshua Olson

Library of Congress Control Number: 2021951398

Publisher's Cataloging-in-Publication Data

Names: Sebra, Richard, author.
Title: California / by Richard Sebra
Description: Minneapolis, Minnesota : Abdo Publishing, 2023 | Series: Core library of US states | Includes online resources and index.
Identifiers: ISBN 9781532197468 (lib. bdg.) | ISBN 9781098270223 (ebook)
Subjects: LCSH: U.S. states--Juvenile literature. | Western States (U.S.)--Juvenile literature. | California--History--Juvenile literature. | Physical geography--United States--Juvenile literature.
Classification: DDC 979.4--dc23

Population demographics broken down by race and ethnicity come from the 2019 census estimate. Population totals come from the 2020 census.

CONTENTS

CHAPTER ONE

THE GOLDEN STATE

A plane touches down at Los Angeles International Airport. For the visitors to the Golden State, there is plenty to see and do within just a few miles of the airport. They can lounge on the beach, see the entertainment capital Hollywood, go surfing, and plenty more.

But Los Angeles can be just the starting point of a visit to California. Head north to San Francisco to see the Golden Gate Bridge.

The Golden Gate Bridge is a popular attraction in San Francisco.

Head east from there to see Yosemite National Park. California has a lot to offer.

California's nickname fits the state in many ways. Gold was discovered there in 1848. Golden fields of poppy flowers grow in the state. California is known for its golden rays of sunshine. San Diego is one of the sunniest major cities in the United States. California also boasts long stretches of golden sand. The state has 840 miles (1,352 km) of coast with the Pacific Ocean. These beaches are a fun part of life for many Californians.

WHAT'S IN A NAME?

Spanish explorers named California, but California is not a Spanish word. The name likely comes from a place in a Spanish novel from the 1500s. The California of that book was a beautiful island. The word *California* itself probably comes from Arabic. *Khalif* is a term for a Muslim leader. Spain was ruled by the Moors, who were Muslim, from the mid-700s to the late 1400s. The author of the novel was probably familiar with the word.

ABOUT CALIFORNIA

California is a huge state. It makes up most of the West Coast of the United States. Oregon borders California to the north. Nevada and Arizona form the eastern border. Mexico borders it to the south, and to the west is the Pacific Ocean. The landscapes differ greatly by region.

PERSPECTIVES

HOMELESSNESS

Because California is such a beautiful state, many people want to live there. In fact, about 1 in 9 Americans lives in California. But 1 in 4 Americans experiencing homelessness lives there too. The need for space and slow housing construction in metro coastal areas have driven up home and rental costs. Because of these and other factors, homelessness has become a crisis in California.

People have lived in what is now California for thousands of years. Approximately 300,000 people lived in the region at the time Europeans first visited. But the state exploded in population with the discovery of gold in 1848 in Sutter Creek. San Francisco grew from a town of 200 in 1846 to 36,000 in 1852. Thousands from across the United States and the world left their homes and loved ones, hoping to strike it rich. Today the San Francisco Bay Area, including San Jose, is home to some of the world's biggest technology companies.

California has been the national leader in agriculture since the early 1900s. It produces nearly half of all the fruits, nuts, and vegetables for the United States. Most of these crops grow in the state's huge Central Valley. That's also where the state capital of Sacramento is located.

Southern California is known for beautiful weather, beaches, and more. Los Angeles is the second-most populous American city. Many films are made there. San Diego is known for surfing. It is also home to one of the main ports of the US Navy. People from all over the world go to California for many reasons. These people have made California the diverse state that it is today.

MAP OF CALIFORNIA

California's four biggest cities are Los Angeles, San Diego, San Jose, and San Francisco. What do you notice about the general location of each of these cities? Why do you think large cities developed there?

CHAPTER TWO

HISTORY OF CALIFORNIA

People have been living in what is now California for at least 19,000 years. The first people to live there came from Asia. Peoples such as the Shasta and Tolowa Dee-ni' have long lived in the northwest. Both the Shasta and the Tolowa Dee-ni' once used giant redwood trees to build boats and homes.

Central California peoples, including the Miwok, live in the Central Valley. The region had a lot of edible plants, which the Miwok

Miwok people in California continue to celebrate their cultures in many ways, including through dance.

maintained and harvested. There were many animals, including salmon, elk, and rabbits. There was enough food to support villages of up to 1,000 people. The Kumeyaay people have long lived in the area that is now San Diego. They fished from the Pacific Ocean and the mountain streams.

EUROPEANS

Spanish explorer Juan Rodriguez Cabrillo met the Kumeyaay when he landed in San Diego Bay in 1542. Cabrillo was the first European to explore California. The Spanish did not have a major presence in the area, which they called New Spain, until 1769. Some worked to convert Indigenous people to Catholicism. The Spanish colonized California. Settlers forced some American Indians off their lands. The Spanish also brought diseases. American Indians had no protection from these diseases. Over the next 65 years, diseases killed approximately half of the American Indians in the area.

People can see a reconstructed historical Miwok village at Indian Grinding Rock State Historic Park.

In 1821 the people of New Spain won their independence from Spain. The territory then came under Mexican rule. California was known as Alta California. This territory covered all of modern-day California as well as several other western states. In 1833 Mexico gave land to white Mexican citizens. These lands became large ranches for cattle. The Spanish

Mexican settlers in Alta California were known as Californios.

Some people in Alta California wanted to have more control over their lives. On June 10, 1846, a group of American settlers near the Northern California city of Sonoma declared California an independent country. This act was known as the Bear Flag Revolt. But the revolt did not last long. It ended on July 9 when the rebels learned the United States was already at war with Mexico in the Mexican–American War (1846–1848). The countries were fighting because the United States had recently taken Texas from Mexico. When the war ended in 1848, Mexico lost Alta California, which then belonged to the United States.

As the war ended, gold was discovered in the northern part of the state. People flooded into California. They came from across the country and world. Nearly 100,000 people arrived in 1849 alone.

California officially became the thirty-first US state the next year on September 9.

CONTINUED GROWTH

People continued to come to California after the gold rush. Within ten years the population was more than 300,000. Workers, mainly from China, came to work on building the Transcontinental Railroad during the 1860s. They faced dangerous conditions and racial discrimination.

Beginning in the 1900s, the farming industry provided a lot of jobs. Manufacturing jobs before and after World War II (1939–1945) provided even more jobs. By 1970 California was the most populous US state.

WATER ISSUES

California's booming population helped grow a powerful economy. But it also made an old problem worse. That problem was access to water. Most growing California cities were hundreds of miles from the nearest water source. The state had to engineer huge projects, such as the Hetch Hetchy dam, to get water to people. This led cities to argue over water supply.

PERSPECTIVES

CESAR CHAVEZ

In the 1950s Mexican and Filipino workers in California's farming industry often had poor working conditions and pay. Cesar Chavez was one of these workers. He tried to make a better life for the workers. Chavez said about farm workers, "The tragic thing is that after they make this tremendous contribution, they don't have any money or any food left for themselves." Chavez organized the farm workers into a union. That way they could fight for better conditions together. Along with activist Dolores Huerta, Chavez cofounded what became United Farm Workers in 1962. It is the largest farm workers union in the country.

More and more people owned cars throughout the first half of the 1900s. In California this led to the development of a huge freeway system. This also created a lot of pollution. California passed strict pollution control laws. The state is known today for its laws to protect the environment.

GOVERNMENT

The California state government looks similar to the US government. There is a state

CALIFORNIA QUICK FACTS

There are many things that make California unique. How do these facts about California help you better understand the state?

Abbreviation: CA
Nickname: The Golden State
Motto: Eureka
Date of statehood: September 9, 1850
Capital: Sacramento
Population: 39,538,223
Area: 163,695 square miles (423,968 sq km)

STATE SYMBOLS

State animal
Grizzly bear

State tree
California redwood

State bird
California quail

State flower
California poppy

legislature that has two bodies. The higher house is called the Senate. The lower house is the Assembly. The legislature writes bills and votes them into law. The executive branch is led by the governor. The governor approves new laws. The judicial branch includes the Supreme Court of California. This branch interprets the laws. One unusual aspect of California's government is ballot propositions. These are questions posed to citizens, who vote yes or no. Propositions allow citizens to have a direct say in government.

Modern California has a diverse population. But the state has struggled with racial discrimination. Black people have lived in California since it became a US state. But many more moved to California between the 1940s and 1970s. Black people have historically faced unequal treatment in housing, jobs, and interactions with police. Large riots took place in both the 1960s and 1990s after Black people were hurt or killed by police. Continually working to fix these problems is part of California's story.

STRAIGHT TO THE SOURCE

Augustin Hibbard came to California in the 1849 gold rush. Hibbard wrote a letter to his brother explaining that the work was hard and the rewards were slim:

> *In [instances], (and rarely it is that they occur) where a man is fortunate enough during the mining season . . . to take out [$50,000] it is trumpeted abroad in such a manner as to give reason to suppose that all in the region . . . are doing about or equally as well. Thus these reports go home, and people come out here [thinking] that they, are certain of doing the same.*
>
> *But alas, how woefully are they disappointed. . . . Not one in 500 make $50000 a year. And not more than one in a hundred, that makes more than his expenses.*

Source: "Letter from Augustin Hibbard to William Hibbard 1850 Sept. 4." *University of the Pacific*, n.d., scholarlycommons.pacific.edu. Accessed 2 Feb. 2021.

BACK IT UP

Hibbard is using evidence to support a point about the reality of gold mining in California. Write a paragraph describing the point Hibbard is making. Then write down two or three pieces of evidence Hibbard uses to make the point.

CHAPTER THREE

GEOGRAPHY AND CLIMATE

California is a land of extremes. It features the highest point in the lower 48 states. The peak of Mount Whitney stands 14,495 feet (4,418 m) high. California also has the lowest point in North America. Death Valley is 282 feet (86 m) below sea level. Both points are located in the same county in east-central California.

California is located on top of two tectonic plates. These plates are large blocks of Earth's crust. They move slowly, pushing against

Few plants grow in parts of Death Valley.

one another. The area where plates meet is called a fault. The largest fault in California is the San Andreas Fault. It runs through most of the state from north to south.

Plates pushed against each other, causing the land to rise. This movement of tectonic plates formed mountains in the state. The high Sierra Nevada lie in the north and east. The Pacific Coast Ranges in the west run down to the Pacific Ocean.

California's size means it has many climates. Inland deserts are hot and dry. Death Valley is among the hottest

PERSPECTIVES

RYAN CONRADI

Sonoma County park ranger Ryan Conradi is one of the people protecting California's natural beauty. As a ranger, he gives directions, cleans up litter, helps people in trouble, leads teaching programs, and more. Conradi said to the *Sonoma West Times and News*, "I would say one of my favorite things is just to walk around and greet people and make sure people are having a good time."

places in the world, with summer temperatures often hitting 120 degrees Fahrenheit (49°C) or above. Higher elevation areas are cool and get snow in winter. California's lowest temperature was recorded high in the Sierra Nevada. It reached −45 degrees Fahrenheit (−43°C) on January 20, 1937. Coastal areas tend to be mild year-round.

Driving to all of California's different landscapes would take days. The trip would cover snowy peaks, hot deserts, and sandy beaches. Few other states have so many types of geography.

PLANTS AND ANIMALS

The Pacific Ocean is a big part of life in California. It is home to many creatures. Sea otters, seals, and sea lions are common sights in California harbors. Pelicans and gulls soar above the coast. A little farther into the ocean are whales. Black bears, coyotes, and elk are among the species found inland. The California condor soars in the southwestern skies in mountainous regions.

Sea lions often rest on Pier 39 in San Francisco.

California has many unique trees. It is common to see evergreen trees at high elevations. The largest of these are sequoias. Redwoods grow closer to the coast. These trees reach hundreds of feet high. Palm trees can be found across the state. The one native palm species, the California fan palm, is found in deserts in Southern California.

CLIMATE THREATS

Climate change refers to the rising average temperatures of Earth. This increased warming comes from pollution and other factors caused by humans. Climate change poses many threats to California. Coastal areas are at risk of flooding from rising sea levels. Higher temperatures lead to dry weather. This increases the risk of destructive wildfires. Fires can happen anytime. But historically they are most common from May to October. California's rainy season once began in November. But the rainy season now starts

SEQUOIAS AND REDWOODS

Giant sequoias and redwoods are two closely related species of trees. Both live only in California. Both are huge in different ways. The sequoia is the largest tree in the world. Its base can be 100 feet (30 m) around. Sequoias have grown up to 311 feet (95 m) tall. The redwood is slimmer than the sequoia. But it is taller. The tallest one on record stood 378 feet (115 m) tall. There are redwoods with holes so wide that people can drive through.

Wildfires damage homes and animal habitats.

nearly a month later than it used to. This makes the fire season even longer.

In addition the state endured a drought from 2011 to 2019. At its peak, approximately 60 percent of the state experienced the most severe level of drought. At that level, crop harvest is very low. Wildfires start easily and do a lot of damage.

California is also at risk of earthquakes. The tectonic plates that meet at the San Andreas Fault can create powerful earthquakes when they rub together. The state has experienced some of the biggest earthquakes in US history. A 1906 earthquake near San Francisco killed 3,000 people across the Bay Area. San Francisco was almost completely destroyed. The quake measured 7.9

on the Richter scale. The strongest earthquake ever measured in the world was 9.5.

A 1994 earthquake hit the Northridge neighborhood of Los Angeles. It killed 60 people. Scientists didn't know that a fault line existed there, so most of the buildings were not designed to withstand a quake. This led to changes in laws about how to build more safely. Earthquakes will always be a threat to the Golden State. In the early 2000s, scientists predicted California was due for another major earthquake along the San Andreas Fault in the next 30 years.

EXPLORE ONLINE

Chapter Three discusses some of the effects of climate change on California, including increasing wildfires. The article at the website below goes into more depth on this topic. Does the article answer any of the questions you had about climate change in California?

WILDFIRES

abdocorelibrary.com/california

CHAPTER FOUR

RESOURCES AND ECONOMY

California is big in many ways, including economically. If California were its own country, it would have the fifth-largest economy in the world. California is home to many huge industries.

Gold attracted many people to California in the 1840s. Gold mining is no longer a major industry. But California still depends on its natural resources. Farming is important. The state produces more than 400 different products, including avocados, beef, dairy

Agriculture, including growing crops such as almonds, is a big industry in California.

products, and many kinds of nuts from almonds to walnuts.

California moves a lot of goods. The combined port of Los Angeles and Long Beach is the busiest port in the Americas. It processes nearly 18 million shipping containers per year. The port of Oakland is also one of the top 15 busiest.

IMMIGRANT WORKFORCE

Immigrants have come to California for centuries looking for work. Today one in three California workers is an immigrant. The industry with the most immigrant workers is manufacturing, followed closely by health care. The industry with the largest percentage of immigrant workers is agriculture. Sixty-three percent of those employees are immigrants. Immigrant families contribute nearly $40 billion in taxes to the state's economy.

BUSINESS AND FILM

Northern California is a hub for business. The center of the technology industry is called Silicon Valley. It is located in the San Francisco Bay Area.

Cupertino, California, is the location of Apple's headquarters.

Companies such as Apple and Google began in Silicon Valley. They still have their global headquarters there. And they have been joined by many others.

California's sunny weather makes it an ideal home for the entertainment industry. Filmmakers can make movies there all year. Today the film industry brings billions of dollars into California. The industry is centered around Hollywood, a district of Los Angeles.

California's sunny weather also helped create another industry. The state has the largest solar power industry in the country. Solar provides 20 percent of California's energy.

From national parks to beaches, California has many places people love to visit. Tourists spent more than $140 billion visiting California

PERSPECTIVES

CARL LAEMMLE

Carl Laemmle was born in Germany in 1867. In 1884 he moved to the United States. At the age of 40, he got into the movie business. While operating his first film studio in New York, Laemmle had the idea for a "movie city." This eventually became Universal Studios. It opened in the San Fernando Valley in Los Angeles County in 1915. Laemmle was one of the first film producers to be based in Southern California. Laemmle also had the idea to sell tickets to the public so they could see movies being made. Universal Studios still gives tours today. It also has a theme park.

People can tour the Paramount film studio in Hollywood.

in 2019. The tourism industry employed 1.2 million Californians. California has a lot of things to offer, making its economy large.

FURTHER EVIDENCE

Chapter Four provides an overview of California's economy, including the film industry. What was one of the main points of this chapter? What evidence is included to support this point? Read the article at the website below. Does the information on the website support the main point of the chapter? Does it present new evidence?

WHERE IS HOLLYWOOD?

abdocorelibrary.com/california

Far East CAFÉ
EAFOOD CUISINE
KARAOKE
Grant AVE. Tel.(415)982-3245
l Mountain
onastery
OLD SHANGHAI
HOME DECOR & ORIENTAL FASHION
BAZAAR
Bank of
銀行
SACRAMENTO
NO PARKING

CHAPTER FIVE

PEOPLE AND PLACES

Many famous people come from California. *Black Panther* director Ryan Coogler is from Oakland. So is singer and actress Zendaya. Joe DiMaggio, one of the greatest baseball players of all time, was born in Martinez.

California is full of many notable landmarks. The Golden Gate Bridge is located in San Francisco. It is one of California's world-famous landmarks. It was also one of

People enjoy dining at the many Chinese restaurants in San Francisco's Chinatown.

the first sights that immigrants saw coming to California.

Immigrants have shaped the history of California. Before the Golden Gate Bridge was built, immigrants from China formed San Francisco's Chinatown. Many Mexicans moved to California in the 1900s for work, especially in agriculture. Today Mexican Americans work in all industries. Because Mexican culture is such a big part of California's culture, many people of all backgrounds get to enjoy Mexican food, music, and art throughout the state.

PERSPECTIVES

KAMALA HARRIS

Politician Kamala Harris was born in Oakland to a Jamaican father and an Indian mother. Harris went into law. In 2011 she became the state's attorney general. She was the first Black American elected to the office. Six years later, she became the second Black woman and first Indian American elected to the US Senate. Harris's history of fighting for social justice earned her the Democratic nomination for vice president in 2020. She became the first female vice president when she took office in 2021.

Many restaurants in California serve food inspired by Mexican cuisine.

Hispanic and Latino people are now the largest ethnic group in California. They make up 39.4 percent of the state's population. White people who are not Hispanic or Latino make up 36.5 percent. Asian people make up 15.5 percent, Black people are 6.5 percent, and American Indians make up 1.6 percent. California today has the largest American Indian population in the United States at more than 700,000. There are more than 100 federally recognized American Indian tribes in the state. These tribes and nations have their own governments.

All immigrant groups have helped make California what it is today. The influence of immigration has made

Many people enjoy hiking in Yosemite to see Half Dome.

the state diverse. California has become a blend of old and new traditions.

LANDMARKS AND FUN

Many of the most famous landmarks in the United States are in California. Besides seeing the Golden Gate Bridge, visitors to San Francisco may enjoy taking a ride on a cable car. East from the Bay Area is Yosemite

National Park. It is home to Half Dome. This granite dome stands nearly 5,000 feet (1,500 m) above the valley floor below.

Mount Shasta, one of the state's tallest peaks, is near the northern border with Oregon. The region is dotted with national forests. These are popular destinations for people looking to hike and camp.

Southern California is known for beaches, surfing, and Hollywood. It's also home to natural wonders such as Joshua Tree National

NEW PRO SPORTS FRONTIER

For the first half of the 1900s, US professional sports teams were mostly in the Northeast and Midwest. California was the new frontier for teams as the state's population exploded in the mid-1900s. The Cleveland Rams football team moved to Los Angeles in 1946. The San Francisco 49ers football team began playing the same year. But the biggest move came from two baseball teams in 1958. The Brooklyn Dodgers and New York Giants were two of the top teams in Major League Baseball. Their move to California kick-started a westward expansion of baseball.

Surfing is a popular activity in California.

Park. World-class concerts take place at the Hollywood Bowl outdoor theater. And for sports fans, the Los Angeles area is home to at least one team in every major professional sport.

Gold may have brought people to California many years ago. But there are other things that have kept people coming for generations since. Whether it's the sun, sand, scenery, or something else, California has an adventure for everyone.

STRAIGHT TO THE SOURCE

Brian De Los Santos, born in Mexico but raised in Los Angeles, explained his experience growing up in the United States:

> *Being a Latino in the US can sometimes mean an evolving sense of identity. When I was a child, . . . I thought being American meant reciting the Pledge of Allegiance, learning about the War of 1812 in history class and watching blockbuster hits with friends. But being at home was living in another world.*
>
> *Ma would cook* enchiladas en salsa verde *and, at least once a week, would shove the phone in my face,* "Ten, habla con tu abuela que te quiere oír." *Translation: My grandma wanted to hear my voice. . . .*
>
> *I loved being in two worlds. . . . I'm not just one thing—and, ultimately, being Latino isn't one specific experience either.*

Source: Brian De Los Santos. "For Me, Being Latino Means Living between Two Worlds." *Los Angeles Times*, 16 Sept. 2016, latimes.com. Accessed 2 Feb. 2021.

WHAT'S THE BIG IDEA?

Take a close look at this passage. What is the main point De Los Santos is making about his experience? Find two or three details used to support that main point.

IMPORTANT DATES

19,000 years ago (approximately)
People begin living in what is now California.

1542
Spanish explorer Juan Rodriguez Cabrillo becomes the first European to visit what is now California.

1821
The territory of New Spain, including what is now California, wins its independence from Spain. The territory comes under Mexican rule.

1848
Gold is discovered, sparking a huge gold rush that brings hundreds of thousands of people to California. The Mexican–American War ends, and what is now California becomes a part of the United States.

1849
Nearly 100,000 people arrive in California during the gold rush.

1850
California becomes the thirty-first US state.

1906
A huge earthquake destroys much of San Francisco and kills 3,000 people throughout the area.

1970
California becomes the most populous US state.

2011–2019
A long drought hits California.

STOP AND THINK

Surprise Me

Chapter Three discusses the geography of California. After reading this book, what two or three facts about California's geography did you find most surprising? Write a few sentences about each fact. Why did you find each fact surprising?

Say What?

Studying the history of a state can mean learning a lot of new vocabulary. Find five words in this book you've never heard before. Use a dictionary to find out what they mean. Then write the meanings in your own words and use each word in a new sentence.

You Are There

This book describes some things to see in San Francisco. Imagine you are a tourist in San Francisco. Write a letter home telling your friends what you have seen. What place did you find most interesting? Be sure to add plenty of detail to your notes.

Another View

This book talks about the hardships that American Indian people endured with the arrival of Europeans. As you know, every source is different. Ask a librarian or another adult to help you find another source about this topic. Write a short essay comparing and contrasting the new source's point of view with that of this book's author. What is the point of view of each author? How are they similar and why? How are they different and why?

GLOSSARY

climate
the general weather conditions of a certain region

colonize
to move into and take control of a new place

crop
a plant grown to be used as food

economy
a place's system of goods, services, money, and jobs

independent
able to make decisions without being controlled by another party

territory
an area of land that is not a state but is still controlled by a country

union
an organization of workers from a certain industry that promotes the workers' interests

ONLINE RESOURCES

To learn more about California, visit our free resource websites below.

Core Library CONNECTION
FREE! COMMON CORE MULTIMEDIA RESOURCES

Visit **abdocorelibrary.com** or scan this QR code for free Common Core resources for teachers and students, including vetted activities, multimedia, and booklinks, for deeper subject comprehension.

Booklinks NONFICTION NETWORK
FREE! ONLINE NONFICTION RESOURCES

Visit **abdobooklinks.com** or scan this QR code for free additional online weblinks for further learning. These links are routinely monitored and updated to provide the most current information available.

LEARN MORE

London, Martha. *The Effects of Climate Change*. Abdo, 2021.

Seigel, Rachel. *California and Other Western Wildfires*. Crabtree, 2019.

Yasuda, Anita. *Exploring the West*. Abdo, 2018.

INDEX

About the Author

Richard Sebra is a children's book author and journalist. He and his wife enjoy cooking, surfing, and hiking with their dogs.